Life Warrior

The Everyday Summit

Karolee Krause, LPC, SAC

To those who climb

About the Author

Karolee Krause is a clinical consultant, Licensed Professional Counselor, and author with extensive experience in the areas of leadership, personal development, spiritual growth, and addictions and recovery.

Karolee is certified as an art therapist, advanced mindfulness leader, qigong instructor, drum circle facilitator and laughter yoga leader.

Karolee is passionate about helping people through career changes and life transitions.

Table of Contents

Introduction 11
Preface 17
Preparing to Climb 19
    Obstacles 22
    Base Camps 23
    Rewards 24
    Tools for the Journey 25
    Mission 26
    Preparations 26
    Flags 28
    Rest Spots 31
The Way of the Warrior 33
Home Base 39
Base Camp 1 47
Base Camp 2 69
Base Camp 3 87
Base Camp 4 111
Base Camp 5 131
Base Camp 6 149
Base Camp 7 169
The Summit 183

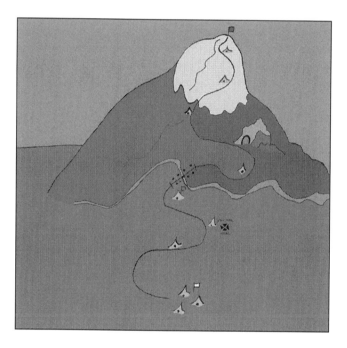

The Warrior's Map to the Summit

Introduction

Life Warrior, The Everyday Summit was written as a motivational self-help guide and personal success book in which you will take the journey of your lifetime, of becoming a leader and warrior within.

You are about to embark on one of the most rewarding and challenging adventures you have ever taken. Throughout the journey, you will discover personal strengths and skills you did not know you had. You will find magical talismans and special potions that will empower and help you get to the next base camp, and ultimately to the summit at the top of the mountain.

In *Life Warrior, The Everyday Summit*, you will climb over enormous boulders, hike up steep, jagged rocks, cross barren deserts, swim across raging rivers, and crawl through dark bat filled caves. The adventure is not for the weak of mind, spirit, or body, but for those with the bravery to accept the challenge to reach the summit.

As a warrior, your journey is a solo one in which you will commit to a new path, one of personal strength and power that will ultimately lead to a new life.

As warrior, you will need to leave behind old, negative life patterns, false beliefs, and destructive life cycles, as you learn to gain mastery over your own life.

This is the adventure that awaits you as a warrior.

Climbing the mountain won't be without its struggles. As in daily life, we are all faced with difficult, nearly impossible choices and decisions. The difference between you and others is that as a warrior you know that when you reach the summit, you will never want to return to life as you once knew it because you will have learned to face difficult decisions with courage in your heart.

Part of your journey will involve using the weapons and tools that you will gather on your adventure. You will use them to overcome the challenges of everyday life.

Never forget that warriors are relentlessly tested as they commit to personal goals to reach the summit. Through emotional and mental strength, spiritual guidance, and physical endurance, the warrior ultimately reaches his or her true destination: the self.

As you prepare for the journey of a lifetime, remember that becoming a warrior means releasing the past, facing unknown fears and uncertainties, saying goodbye to familiar people, and stepping onto an unknown and unfamiliar path. This is not an adventure for the faint of heart.

The rewards are great: a warrior's path leads to wholeness.

You will not be completely alone on your ascent to the summit because warriors are guided every step of the way, though always remembering that their strongest guide is their own inner wisdom.

Life presents many pathways and so too will this journey. Every day there is an opportunity to step outside of repetitive and familiar patterns, unhealthy habits, and dead-end behaviors. A new path, the warrior's path is about to begin. If you are ready, this moment offers you a new journey, one that will change your life forever.

Preface

Life Warrior, The Everyday Summit was inspired by life lessons learned personally and professionally in which adversity had to be overcome.

Life presents us with challenges and encompasses disappointments or loss in the areas of career change, life transitions, relationship conflict, grief and loss or even in everyday stress management.

Life Warrior, The Everyday Summit was written to inspire those who are brave enough to climb the summit each and every day, knowing that a better life awaits them.

Preparing to Climb

Throughout your journey to the summit, you will be offered several survival tools and specific guidance every step of the way. Your mission will be to find and collect essential tools, and to search out symbolic messages that are hidden in the landscape to help you stay on the warrior's path and ultimately reach the summit.

The obstacles and challenges that you will encounter as warrior, along with the tools, talismans, and magical potions that you will find throughout the journey are described below.

Obstacles

The path to the summit will often appear flat and easy to navigate in the beginning of your journey, but it will quickly change and become steeper and more difficult to climb.

You will have to cross a fast-flowing, rock-strewn, and treacherous river in order to reach the other side. Even then, cold and wet, you will seek shelter from natural elements like torrential rain and thunderstorms.

You will enter and crawl through dark, narrow bat filled caves that will strike terror to the very core of your being. Turning back will no longer be an option at this point, but you will not want to return to your old way of life. No matter how difficult the journey, you renew an oath to yourself to move forward, up the side of the mountain.

Base Camps

A dangerous and lengthy journey, you will not ascend to the summit easily or in one short day. You will be aided by a series of base camps that will allow you to rest, restore your mind, body, and spirit as the journey provides you with ever greater challenges.

Base camps, however, are not home, and you will never stay at any one of them for very long—forcing yourself to continue in your quest for the top.

Rewards

Talismans and magical potions are hidden from view in a variety of locations throughout your journey. These items will give you strength and endurance to help you get to the next base camp and ultimately to your final destination: the mountain's summit.

You will also find spiritual messages and guidance along your journey, but only if you look carefully and in the right places.

Messages may be carved on desert rocks or appear silently in the clouds above. Spiritual guidance will encourage you to continue the warrior's journey and guide you every step of the way—but only if you are willing to seek it out.

Tools for the Journey

Emotional, mental, and physical self-care tools will be found at each base camp along the way. These tools are not always easy to find, but once found, they will be lifesaving.

Mission

Your mission is to become the warrior within, to rise above everyday problems, and overcome lifelong negative self-sabotaging patterns of behavior and to become the master of your true authentic self.

Preparations

At each base camp, you must take inventory of what you need to leave behind including past regrets, self-loathing, blame, dependency, codependency, addictions, anger, maladaptive patterns, hatred, jealousy, resentment, toxic thinking patterns, and any form of destructive energy that keeps you stuck in a negative life cycle.

The warrior's path will be filled with slippery rocks and dangerous curves, but what is more dangerous than the trail itself is fear, both fear of the journey and fear of failure in not reaching the summit.

The warrior must abandon all fear of the journey because if she or he does not, the warrior will not succeed.

Fear will always return as the warrior's climb gains in elevation. Sometimes the fear will seem paralyzing and can take many forms, including slipping and falling off the mountain, of not making it to the summit, or of being alone on the journey.

What sets warriors apart is not that they don't feel fear, but they don't dwell on it. Warriors learn to overcome their fears.

Flags

Along your journey, you will discover three flags, each located at key locations in your journey to the summit. The first flag will be found at home base, the next at the half-way point in the journey, and the final flag is planted at the summit. The three flags and their colors represent aspects of your journey including white for surrender, which marks the beginning of the journey and your willingness to surrender your old life and old ways of being as you accept the journey and make a commitment to change.

The second flag along the way is red and located at the midpoint of the journey. Halfway up the mountain, you will find yourself in a transitional place where you must make the decision to continue to climb to the summit, although difficult and painful at times. Or you can make the decision to go back down the mountain to the old life you left behind. But when you make the choice to continue, you will have to fully commit to your journey to the summit.

The red flag represents both power and danger, depending on your choice to continue to the summit or return to the life you left behind in the past.

The final flag in your journey is purple. This flag is located on the mountain's summit and represents spiritual conquest. As you reach the end of your journey, you will be bestowed with spiritual wisdom and direction as you continue your life forward as a newfound warrior.

Rest Spots

Along the way, you will need to search for places to rest and replenish your body, mind, and spirit. Although you will depend upon the base camps, you will also find caves and alcoves to rest in. At other times you may have to build your own shelter from the resources around you. As in life, we won't always have retreats or base camps to go to and we will have to create our own.

The Way of the Warrior

Home base is your familiar present-day life situation. You recognize many people, but like you, most of them are discontent with their daily lives. You have spent years, possibly a lifetime at home base but you also know that to stay would mean to stagnate and die.

Although familiar, you have outgrown many of the people in your life, and many aspects of home no longer resonate with you. You know that a better life exists elsewhere, so you make the decision to leave behind what no longer serves you as you prepare for the most important journey of your lifetime.

As a warrior you know that you will meet with resistance on your journey as others may not understand your mission or respect your desire for change. Others will make attempts to throw the warrior off their path but the warrior understands that others are threatened by the warrior's decision to move on. As the warrior, you continue to make plans to depart on your journey to a better life.

Warriors have to make difficult decisions at times, and sometimes the choice must be to leave unhealthy people and situations behind. The warrior recognizes, however, that those choices are made out of love, both love for self, and love for others.

You begin to prepare to leave your home and enter the unknown, leaving everything that no longer serves you behind.

Home Base

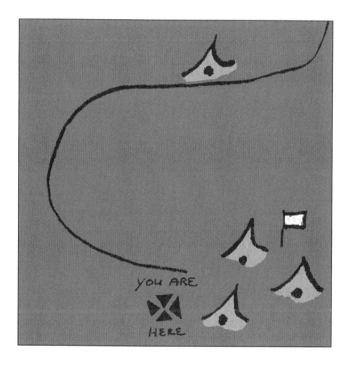

Home Base: Your Journey Begins

You are a warrior, standing at the base of a sacred mountain. You have already traveled long and far, yet you know the journey is really just beginning. You are driven to climb the mountain because you know that the journey to the summit is also a journey within, to your true home.

You are already weary as you have traveled a lifetime just to reach the base of the mountain. The journey has not been easy, and yet you know that the hardest part of the journey lies ahead.

You stand next to the white flag at home base. You know that the flag represents surrender and to make the journey of the warrior, you must surrender everything, your past, your future expectations, and what no longer serves you.

As you stand in the near complete darkness of early morning, you see the summit shining brightly above you in the distance. Although people surround you, they are lost and directionless, stumbling to find their own way.

You know that you must make the journey to the summit yourself as it will lead to your authentic self. All other journeys are meaningless and will lead nowhere.

The journey to self will be worth the difficult climb.

With a single, first step, you move tentatively forward and upward, leaving the others behind to live their lives in darkness.

The warrior's quest is to travel to the mountaintop and reach the summit. Along the way, the warrior needs to be aware that she or he will face many obstacles and challenges. The warrior acknowledges this, but still does not question the path. They simply trust that they are being guided. Warriors begin their journey prepared for the adventures and adversities that life brings, and they offer thanks. With a single step, they begin to climb the mountain, with the understanding that the long, difficult, and beautiful journey leads back to the self. The summit is their home within.

Base Camp 1

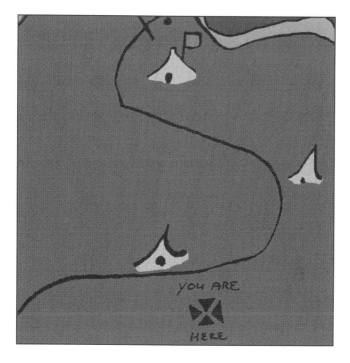

Base Camp 1: Commitment to Change

You begin the journey with nothing but a promise and commitment to yourself that you will reach the summit, so you make the decision to climb. You say your goodbyes and leave everything behind.

The path is enjoyable at first. Each footstep feels right and is effortless as it leads you out of the darkness and shadow of the mountain. The summit is visible and appears to not be that far away. But this is an illusion.

As the path slowly starts to increase in altitude, small rocks begin to appear on the path. They are easy enough to step over as you continue your ascent.

After walking for several hours, you notice that the sun is directly overhead. It warms your body and reassures your soul that you are on the right path.

The warrior begins the day giving thanks for a new beginning. You are grateful for your first breath of the day, reminding yourself that you are alive. The warrior enters the day with optimism and hope.

You observe the mountain as you continue to walk, noting its power and strength. The warrior knows that there is no turning back once the journey has begun otherwise if they did, the past would hold them hostage. You keep climbing and pressing forward.

You seek sacredness, not only in your journey, but in everyday life.

As the path becomes steeper, your backpack grows heavier.

The mountain grows ever more silent, yet you start to hear internal voices telling you to turn back. Some of the voices are not your own so you ignore those voices and listen to your own inner voice growing stronger, telling you to continue your journey. With growing resolve, you march onward and upward.

Hours slowly pass as the terrain begins to change. You leave tracks in the dusty red earth with every step. Rocks and boulders appear more frequently on the path, but your mind is clear. You feel confident in your decision to climb to the summit and are mindful of the path ahead.

You contemplate the life you left behind as you hike the mountain trail, but you begin to grow tired and feel the need to search for a place to rest. There is nothing around you but barren desert. Silent cacti scattered across the ancient landscape seem to resent your presence as you toss your backpack onto the dusty earth and sit down. You look at the path and the life that you have left behind and question if you should return to home base, but you know that there is nothing there for you anymore. At this point, you resist the voices to return as optimism for a better life pulls you forward.

You stand up and dust the dirt off your pants when you notice something on the rock next to you. Carved deeply into the crystalized red sandstone is a symbol that you do not understand. It appears to be three triangles. You know that the symbol is ancient and has meaning, but you do not understand its significance. You note the symbol and continue along the trail.

The path grows steeper and the scenery more beautiful as you continue up the mountain side.

By midday you again grow weary and have thoughts of quitting but recognize these thoughts as self-sabotage you keep moving.

Exhaustion begins to settle in after hours of climbing, and the sun begins to quickly set. You become fearful as you know you need to reach the next base camp before nightfall. Then you see a fork in the path ahead. You have no idea which way to go. You panic as you contemplate what to do. Your instinct is to run down the mountain to safety, to your old familiar life, although an unhappy one. Somehow you resist the urge to go back.

Although both paths look similar, upon closer observation, one appears to be more inviting and looks to be an easier path to follow. Knowing that life often presents itself as paradox, what appears to be easy, will be difficult, and what appears hard will be easy. With this knowledge, you are mindful not to merely take the easy path.

Dust swirls around your feet, as the wind begins to pick up in speed and intensity. You contemplate which path to take as the wrong path could lead you away from the next base camp and into danger.

You look around and realize that you are alone, completely alone. You intuitively know that you have to be still and listen in order to hear the wind, as it may hold a message for you as to which way to go.

Quietly and subtly, the wind shifts and changes direction as it blows westward. The warrior understands the unseen power and forces of nature. You know that the wind guides you westward, so you take the path to your right, trusting that the winds of change will bring you to your next destination.

Although you are weary, you continue to climb. The terrain changes and becomes increasingly alien to you as you walk in mindfulness being aware of each step and every breath you take. You simply focus on the world that surrounds you.

Just as the sun begins to set, you spot the next base camp in the distance. You pick up the pace and follow the narrowing trail, feeling a sense of relief. You do not see a tent or shelter to sleep in and must build your own shelter for the night. You are exhausted, and frustrated.

The last thing you wanted to do is build a shelter for yourself. You become angry. Your emotions overwhelm you as you stomp around the makeshift camp looking for branches and other material. You are furious but then stop in your tracks. You stand still in the moment before again focusing on the task at hand and will the anger to leave your body. It's ok you tell yourself. It's just a part of life. Warriors do not have expectations that things will always go the way that they want them to. Although difficult and challenging, they also know there will be times when they will be forced to create new lives, new homes, and new jobs.

You calm yourself, take a deep breath calling back your energy and continue to gather wooden sticks and begin to construct a small shelter.

Someone has left an old ragged tarp behind, so you use that for a roof. After a short period of time, you have built your temporary home and crawl inside it, exhausted. You give thanks. You have made it to your first destination.

Inside your newly built shelter, you remember that you are not the only person in base camp. There are a few others who are also making their own personal pilgrimage to the summit. You know that some of the others will make it to the top, and others won't. Like you, they are all searching for purpose and meaning in their lives.

The first base camp is located on the edge of a forest. Ponderosa pine trees, a familiar sight and scent to you, reminds you of home. You feel a brief moment of weakness, but you don't allow your mind to sabotage you. You focus your mind on the mountain's beauty and tell yourself that you are in the process of creating a new life for yourself.

You unpack your bag, eat dinner and unroll your sleeping bag. Your shelter is small but comfortable enough. A slight wind blows but eases your mind as you drift off into a deep sleep, allowing your body to heal and repair from the day's journey.

At midnight, you wake up with a jolt. Your mind is racing, and you panic. You quickly crawl out of your shelter and into the cool night air.

You take a deep breath and try to center yourself. Base camp is silent. The night is darker than the darkest of nights that you remember. Your mind bombards you with a thousand questions.

Why did you leave home? What are you seeking? What if leaving was a mistake? Will you make it to the summit? Will you succeed? Will you fail? The questions swirl in your head and keep you from the sleep you so desperately need.

Not uncommon when making life changes, you hear old negative voices from the past, tempting you to abandon your new way of life and return to old ways. However, the warrior recognizes this self-sabotage and begins a positive self-dialogue that shifts the destructive energy and self-doubt.

You remind yourself of your commitment to change and feel a returning sense of peace and the panic subsides. You give thanks to the universal spirit that continues to guide you and reminds you that you are not alone on this earthly journey.

You settle back into your makeshift shelter and quickly fall back to sleep, knowing that tomorrow will be a new day and you will continue on your warrior's path.

A Warrior's Checklist

 Commitment to Change

Identify areas in your life that need to change:

- Toxic relationships
- Negative emotions
- Addictions
- Unhealthy behaviors
- Unproductive thinking patterns

Select one item from your list on which you most need to work

Base Camp 2

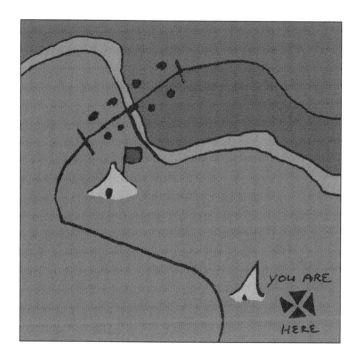

Base Camp 2: Path of Transformation

You search carefully for the path that leads out of the base camp and immediately spot a hidden trail between two juniper trees. The path is somewhat hidden and overgrown, yet still visible. Unlike yesterday's path, it leads away from the slot canyons and into open flat desert terrain, providing a welcome break from the strenuous climb of the day before. The mountain appears to have briefly plateaued, but this is a temporary respite as the hardest part of the journey is yet to come.

    From here, there are no right or wrong paths, as each warrior's journey is individual and unique.

No two paths to the mountain's summit will be the same, nor should they.

Sometimes several pathways are necessary and part of the journey. Warriors recognize this truth, and when walking a dangerous or unstable path, they reroute themselves to safety on another path to quickly avoid potential pitfalls that may lie ahead.

As you hike into unfamiliar territory, you become increasingly aware of your breathing. Your breath, a significant source of energy brings new life into your body, igniting every cell of your being. When exhaled, toxic or stale energy is released, keeping the body in a constant state of equilibrium.

After hiking for hours, the sun has risen directly overhead and you feel the heat of the land rising up in waves from the ground. You stop for a drink of water and notice something move beneath your feet. You look closer and see that it is a beautiful translucent blue snake. You instinctually jump out of the way. Then you face your fears and take a closer look. The snake is not venomous, but a harmless creature that has wandered out of its hole to greet you on your journey.

You become enchanted with the beautiful, hypnotic creature and decide to follow it as it slithers off the path and out into the open desert.

You follow the snake, unconcerned with diverging from your path because the warrior intuitively knows that life is meant to be explored. New experiences and adventures are often found off the beaten path.

The snake travels quickly as it slithers swiftly across the hot desert sand. You continue to follow the snake trusting that you are being guided purposefully in a new direction.

You hike up and down the sand dunes following the snake who appears to be leading you further into the desert and away from your intended path.

Quite quickly and unexpectedly, the snake disappears down a narrow, dark hole leaving you standing alone in the burning sun.

You experience a moment of fear as old negative thought patterns emerge. You question why you have diverted from the original path. Did the snake trick you?

Like the snake, your energy spirals back and forth, emotions rise and then fall, but you trust that you were guided off the path for a reason. You release your fears into the desert wind and begin to look for a new trail.

Like the snake, you will shed your old ways, your old thinking patterns, and negative behaviors as you begin a new life. You also know that like the snake, as you shed, you will be vulnerable. You will need warrior tools and weapons to keep yourself safe, until you reach the summit.

You leave the snake behind, offering gratitude for its guidance before you continue on your way. The landscape that surrounds you is beautiful. Violet cactus flowers are in bloom and the air smells fresh, although dry. Blue skies are dotted with cumulous clouds and you feel a sense of inner peace and calm.

After several hours, your feet grow tired and you begin to doubt you will find your way, but you quickly dismiss the negative self-talk reminding yourself that you are never truly lost.

As you walk, you reflect on the blue snake and its symbolism. Although it was in your life for only a brief time, it reminds you of the people who have been a part of your life's journey but that you have left behind.

The warrior knows that the lesson of the blue snake is one of transformation. Life is beautiful, yet painful, when you shed the past and enter a new life transforming the world around you.

You grow thirsty as the desert around you changes, once beautiful and serene, and becomes foreboding and barren. You walk for hours with nothing in sight.

Your water bottle is almost empty. Fear lodges in your throat as you look around at the desolate desert and question the very existence of your life. Why are you here? Not here in the desert, but here on earth? You continue to walk contemplating the reason for your life, but come up with nothing.

A howling coyote brings you back to the present. Fear grips your soul. You thought you were alone in the desert, but you are not. You panic and run. You have no protection, nowhere to hide. You run terrified further into the setting desert sun and then you stop. Are you running away from danger or running into it?

When warriors are faced with danger or potential pitfalls, they resist reacting emotionally and pause to listen to higher guidance as to what to do.

You look around and see nothing yet the howling continues. Tired, thirsty and hot, you slump to the ground, knowing that if you are under attack, you need to know where the attack is coming from. Warriors are rarely if ever, ambushed or caught off guard.

Your hands sink down into the hot desert sand. You question if you are delusional. Are you hearing things? Is the coyote real? You try to clear your mind knowing that the desert can play tricks on the warrior.

You start to pull yourself up off the ground when you feel something buried deep within the sand. As you pull it out, you see that it is a beautiful green stone. It shines brightly in the palm of your hand.

You recognize the stone as peridot and know that it is a powerful gemstone.

Knowing that nothing is coincidental, the stone has great significance.

The beautiful green gem is symbolic of healing. It also protects the one carrying it.

You hold the peridot up to the sun and acknowledge that the gemstone was placed on your path for a reason, to remind you that the warrior has the power to heal.

You tear a leather string from your backpack and tie it around the stone, making a rough cord to wear around your neck.

You no longer hear the coyote howl and realize that the animal was created by your own mind, a figment of your imagination to teach you that fear is an illusion.

You start walking again. Your feet sink deeply into the sand and every step you take becomes harder and heavier, but you carry on.

You sense that base camp is nearby and just as you walk over the last sand dune into the setting sun, you spot a red flag, reminding you that you have made it halfway to the summit on your journey to becoming whole.

A Warrior's Checklist

 Tools for the Journey

Choose an exercise or activity that helps you to center your mind and body. Practice it once every day. Your activity could include:

- Mindfulness
- Breathing exercises
- Yoga
- Dance
- Drumming
- Physical exercise

Base Camp 3

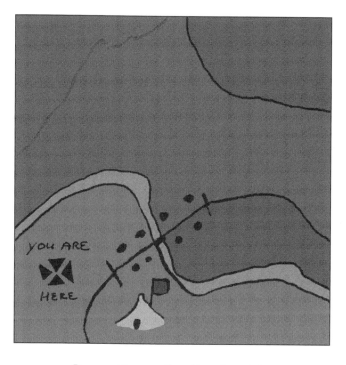

Base Camp 3: Navigating Treacherous Water

You wake up in unfamiliar surroundings and take a deep breath of refreshing mountain air, exhaling yesterday's stale energy. The past is behind you. You are grateful for a new day and a new beginning.

You stand in silence, observing the day as the rosy-colored sun rises over the mountaintop. You have never seen such beauty before. You bow to the rising sun and ask that it keep you warm as you journey throughout the day.

You reflect upon the red flag that marks the halfway point in your journey. You know that red represents power and strength, but it also represents danger as there is a risk that you could turn and go back down the mountain.

Choosing to focus on strength, you focus your mind on the journey ahead.

You prepare your body for the next long leg of the adventure. As warrior, you know that taking care of your physical body is essential to your success. Without a healthy body, the mind is negatively affected. As you continue your climb to the summit, you will need to be strong in body, mind, and spirit.

Warriors listen closely to their body's needs. They know that nutrition, exercise, and rest are essential elements to staying healthy.

The warrior does not disrespect his or her body with alcohol or drugs, nor do they consume unhealthy foods. They do not give in to temptations that sabotage their physical well-being. Instead they make choices that empower their bodies and that create strength and endurance.

As you prepare to leave base camp, you say a prayer of gratitude for the new day. You acknowledge that the journey ahead may be difficult. With that knowledge in mind you step back onto the path.

On the fourth day of your journey, you have thoughts of giving up. Even the strongest and most resolute warrior sometimes experiences moments of weakness.

For warriors who have a past history of addictions, the temptations to use again are great, but with every mindful step, they are reminded of the choices they need to make on a daily basis. During these times, the journey to self is difficult and it feels much easier to return to old familiar ways. The warrior recognizes, though, that she or he is being tested. The warrior knows the pitfalls associated with returning to destructive behaviors and the pain and discontentment that come with those behaviors.

Although their bodies crave the addictions, whether it be drugs, alcohol, food, or other substances or behaviors, warrior spirits become stronger the further they progress along in their journey. The warrior's mission is to hear and respect their body's inner wisdom, and to honor it.

No matter how long they have carried their addiction, warriors make the decision to leave them at the base of the mountain, never to be carried again.

In his or her backpack, healthy and nutritious food and

water are carried, to be consumed throughout the journey. Warriors know that nutrients and hydration are essential. Without strong physical bodies, they won't make it to the summit.

The warrior exercises each day, knowing that the body needs movement to be healthy. A continued focus on health and well-being brings new found energy into every cell of their body.

Back on the mountain path, you settle into solitude. You are not sure of the future or of your path ahead, but you no longer cling to the past. You simply enjoy the present moment. The warrior knows that mental energy spent in the past is wasted and only keeps them tied to a life that no longer exists, so they keep their thoughts on the present time, and they focus on future goals.

The path begins to wind into switchbacks as the trail grows ever steeper and more treacherous. In spite of the danger, you look up into the open sky, feeling a sense of freedom for the first time in your life.

You stop abruptly.

You stand in silence, becoming one with the mountain. You close your eyes and feel the mountain's strength. Mountain wisdom tells you that mountains can be blown up, eroded by time, or have holes cut through straight to their cores. But they remain strong and intact. The mountain reminds you that you are also strong, so you keep moving toward your destination knowing that you have the power and strength to get through this journey. Today, this day, is all that you need to focus on.

After a few hours, you notice a black crow flying overhead. The crow caws at you and you feel compelled to follow it. It leads you deeper into new territory as the mountain steers you into rocky canyon walls. The sandstone is warm from the relentless sun and the winds of a thousand years have chiseled away at the canyon walls.

Although you are fearful, you trust the crow because you know that guidance comes in many shapes and disguises. The crow's intelligence will not lead you astray.

As the bird flies overhead, you continue to follow until it stops and perches on a cliff above. You sit down on a rock and rest, continuing to follow when the crow flies again.

Without warning, storm clouds appear. Eventually, the crow flies swiftly away leaving you alone in the canyon. Huge raindrops begin to fall, welcome after the long stretch of walking in the hot desert sun. Softly they fall at first, but then become heavier and begin to pelt the ground around you.

You panic as water quickly rises around your feet. You stand alone in the narrow canyon walls looking up into the sky. You don't know what to do. Should you go back or should you go forward? The way is unknown, but you believe that the crow was guiding you for a reason so you run further into the unfamiliar canyon, and the walls close in around you.

A bolt of lightning strikes overhead and lights up the

darkened sky. Water continues to rise. Your mind races. Why did you leave home? Why did you follow the crow? What are you truly seeking? Will you ever succeed and make it to the summit?

You start to run faster, although you have no idea what lies ahead. You trip on a rock and fall face first into the fast-flowing water. You pick yourself up, and start running again, but you have no idea if you are running toward safety or away from it, so you come to an abrupt stop.

The heavens rain down on you and you think it can't get any worse.

You are alone, more alone than you have ever been in your life. You see no way out and start to cry.

You hate your life and start to question why this is happening to you, but then you, the warrior, recognize that negative thoughts carry destructive energy so you shift your thoughts, like the shapeshifter crow, knowing you have both the wisdom and ability to shift yourself out of the current situation.

You choose to run on, as the narrowing slot canyon becomes smaller and smaller. Water rises further as you look up into the sky and see the crow again flying overhead in the stormy dark sky, so you continue to follow.

    The crow leads you around a series of corners and bends until the canyon walls open up and you see shelter ahead, but there is now a dark brown river to cross and raging waters prevent you from reaching the other side.

    You contemplate what to do. You spot an old bridge and make your way to it only to see that it is dilapidated and washed out. Rotted, wooden planks lay all around, so you pick some pieces off of the ground and create a makeshift raft to get you to the opposite bank. You begin to paddle.

After a few strokes the raging water breaks your makeshift raft apart and you fight the current as you grab hold of a remaining wooden board, pull yourself across it, and start to paddle even harder. The water moves you further down the canyon and away from shelter as you try to navigate to shore. Strong currents and swift waters carry you even further away from shelter.

   As panic sets in, you spot the crow overhead riding the tailwinds of the storm. Crow's wisdom tells you to stop fighting the current of the water, so you stop struggling and allow the flow of the fast-flowing river to carry you. Just as you release control, you begin to float to the other side of the river and eventually wash up on shore.

You climb off the wooden board and onto the bank where you start walking toward base camp.

The warrior knows that in life, resistance always leads to suffering and when engaged in a fight, energy is lost and depleted in the sheer act of resisting. The warrior's lesson is to let go and move with the flow of life. Although difficult, attempting to hold onto what no longer is or what no longer serves us, only results in pain.

Cold and wet, you wipe yourself off and say thank you to the crow for guiding you safely to base camp four. The crow leaves you behind as it soars high into the sky and out of sight.

You search for your tent and quickly climb inside to dry off.

You eat your evening meal and again acknowledge others in the camp, but keep to yourself being mindful of your own journey and the lessons you have learned up until this point.

Just as you climb into your sleeping bag, the storm finally passes and you fall into a restful sleep, not knowing what tomorrow will bring or where you will end up, but knowing that this is the way of the warrior.

A Warrior's Checklist

 Relapse Prevention

Recognizing and preventing relapse can take several forms including:

- Recognizing danger
- Identifying where you are losing energy
- Noting addictions, which may include people, drugs, alcohol, food, sex, shopping, or gambling
- Taking care of your physical body
- Identifying triggers
- Self-sabotaging behaviors

Base Camp 4

Base Camp 4: Escaping the Darkness

The next morning you wake to the sounds of the nearby river. It reminds you of your journey the day before. You crawl out of your tent and see that the raging river has subsided. You reflect on life's changes and know that at any moment, life can and will change abruptly, like the raging river that is now a peaceful flowing stream.

You collect your few belongings and pack your bag to begin the next phase of your journey. You search camp for a new trail and fortunately find that the path was not washed out by the storm but remains intact.

You step foot onto the trail and walk into unknown territory. After hours of contemplative hiking, you spot a cave entrance on the horizon. It is nestled deep into shadows of the canyon wall and appears to have been long neglected.

When you reach the cave's entrance, you are unsure what to do. Do you enter the cave? Do you hike around it, or do you turn and go back to the original path?

You light a torch and bravely enter what appears to be an abandoned cave. Nothing but darkness surrounds you, but you see a tunnel that leads further back beyond the entrance of the cave. Should you venture inside or leave the cave and find an alternative way around? Something compels you to enter the cave and explore further.

You walk into the darkness wondering what the cave holds. The silence is deafening. The only thing you hear is your heartbeat which increases with every step.

The tunnel is eerie and unsettling but your torch lights the way. You hike deeper into the cave's interior. Suddenly you trip over a rock and fall down. Your torch flies out of your hand, landing out of reach and burns out. You stumble in the darkness and crawl on your hands and knees in the direction of the torch when your hand lands on a strangely shaped object. You put the item in your pocket and continue to crawl until you finally reach your torch. You struggle to get it relit. When you do, you see that the cave is filled with thousands upon thousands of brown bats. Fear grips you as the bats circle and drop overhead, some of them striking your head. You duck down to the wet ground cowering below the bats.

Panic makes you want to run fleeing. Your force yourself to pause momentarily. Do you continue further into the cave where you believe there may be another way out, or do you go back?

Being a warrior, you quickly get a hold of your fear and summon back your energy. You decide to move forward.

The pale light of the torch barely holds back the darkness which feels like a heavy woolen cloak that covers and threatens to suffocate your body and mind. You are in what feels like the darkest night of your soul. You do not see the way ahead, nor do you see the way back. You are suspended in a void. Terrified, you resist the urge to panic and run; you barely maintain your power and sense of self by remaining still. Your wisdom tells you that if you flee, you could get lost and may never make it out of the cave, so you adjust uncomfortably to the darkness, trusting your inner self. The warrior knows not to make decisions out of haste or fear.

In the darkness you remember the object that you found earlier and reach into your pocket and pull it out. You shine your sputtering torch on what appears to be an ornate glass bottle. It looks to be at least a hundred years old and there are words etched faintly into the glass but they are hard to read. You hold the bottle closer. The word, *Vision* is etched into the glass.

You don't know precisely what the potion is for, but you know as a warrior, that nothing is coincidental and that you are always being guided. Somehow this potion was meant to be found, so you put it back into your pocket and continue carefully making your way further into the dark cave.

The narrow walls feel claustrophobic, but you stay strong as you know that sometimes you have to go through difficult situations to get through to the other side of them. Life was never meant to be without its challenges and for those who hang onto security, they will be challenged in many ways.

The cave is a lonely and scary place. You stumble often on the rocky tunnel floor and then trip and fall, injuring yourself several times. You keep going, regardless. As warrior, you refuse to give up.

After searching for hours in the darkness and with no end in sight, you finally break down. You still can't see the way forward. You trusted your inner vision, but now have doubts you will find your way out of the cave. Fear rises like a raging demon, threatening to engulf your very soul. You question if you are going to die in the cave, forgotten and alone. You fall to your knees and cry. You pray for help, desperate in your prayers.

You have left the past behind and can't see the future. You are terrified. Even as warrior, you have lost your way. You panic and scream for help, but no one hears. Silence surrounds you like an abyss. You are inconsolable as you sob for hours, feeling that God has abandoned you. You question your life's path. Did your life have meaning? What was its purpose? Would it end here, alone in this dark cave?

Exhausted from weeping, you lay down on the ground when you

feel the forgotten bottle inside your jacket. Holding the bottle in your hand, you pry off the stoppered top and make the decision to drink the liquid. You have no idea what it is or what it will do. The potion puts you into a deep sleep where you dream that you travel further into the cave's dark recesses. But you have no fear as you somehow, almost magically, see clearly in the darkness. You move with confidence and trust as you are able to navigate the narrowing cave walls that wind further and deeper into the earth's core.

Your journey, although in darkness, is easy and effortless

as you now see the way ahead. The cave becomes smaller and narrower, but just when you think that the walls are too tight to get through, you finally see a light shining in the distance. You squeeze your way through the most difficult and painful passage out to the other side where there is daylight and a visible path.

You wake up, knowing that the potion provided you with insight and vision to see through the dark illusion of life. You stand up to continue your journey. You trust that the way out lies ahead.

As you walk in darkness, you reflect on the guidance offered by the potion and dream that you had.

The potion was put there for the warrior as a reminder that guidance comes in many forms and shapes. The potion also allowed the warrior to see in the darkness at a time when he or she felt like giving up, reminding them that there is always a way out, even when they are truly lost in the darkness of self-doubt and despair.

You crawl through the cave for several more hours, knowing the darkness is necessary for growth. Painful and frightening as it is, the warrior now has newfound tools to help him or herself through the difficult times in life.

With new hope, you continue on until you see a small circle of light in the distance.

You pick up your pace, careful not to stumble. As you near the light, the cave tunnel finally opens up and illuminates the way out. You squeeze yourself up and out of the cave and fall onto the ground outside. You give gratitude for being guided through the most difficult and dark time of your life.

You stand in the sunlight and look down at the dark cave tunnel at your feet. The cave serves as a reminder of how life's paths will continue to fluctuate and that the warrior will be pulled down into darkness again. But you know that to keep faith, even in the darkness, you will find your way out.

You have lived through the dark night of the soul and survived.

A Warrior's Checklist

 Vision and Insight

Vison and insight come from many sources. Explore how the following might help you discover more about your true inner self:

- Meditation
- Prayer
- Silence
- Time reflecting in nature
- Creative expression
- Study of symbolism or scripture

Base Camp 5

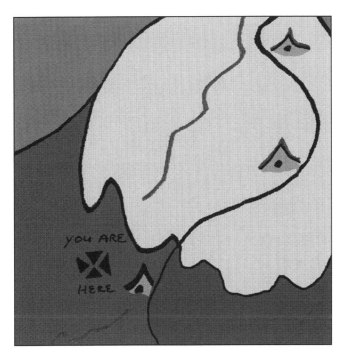

Base Camp 5: Climbing Higher

You reach base camp just as the sun is setting. You see a few people roaming about the small area, but as with previous base camps, the numbers continue to dwindle.

You find an open tent and unpack your bag, feeling the stress and tension release from your aching body.

Before you sleep, you mentally begin to prepare yourself for tomorrow's journey. You have learned that warrior paths are never straight forward or easy, but an ongoing and continuous flow of change.

You remind yourself that the warrior will be tested often when he or she makes the decision to climb to the mountain's summit. You have traveled far, but the tests are not over yet.

The universe will test the warrior in ways that may force her or him to fall off their path and plummet to the steep rocks below, leaving them to re-live old, negative life patterns and emotional cycles.

The warrior will expect that tests lie ahead but will continue to climb, clearly seeing the path both below as well as ahead of them.

Mindfulness is the key to a warrior's success. They are mindful of where their energy is at all times. If they begin to feel depressed, warriors use a variety of tools to energetically shift their energy to higher levels of vibration.

    The warrior is always mindful of the thoughts and words she or he uses. If they hear themselves complaining or being negative, they quickly acknowledge those actions and stop. They learn to reframe what they have said and identify what they are feeling; they use their healing weapons to return to a state of positivity and balance.

    In working through those emotions, the warrior must look for the source of their negative energy and immediately go on the attack, destroying the destructive energy at its source.

Through ongoing mindfulness, the warrior remains in control and makes healthy decisions that keep them strong in body, mind, and spirit as they continue their climb to the summit.

Having prepared yourself for the next day, you sleep well through the night and wake up feeling refreshed. You look forward to the day's journey.

You pick up your backpack and follow the trail out of base camp. You look up into the open blue sky and notice that there is not a cloud in sight.

The trail begins to increase in elevation and the path becomes steeper. You have to pause often for breaks along the way but enjoy the challenge presented by the increasing elevation. You notice a straight, dead branch laying across the path and pick it up. It will become your walking stick and companion for the rest of the journey. Like you, the stick has its own story, even if it remains untold to you.

    The warrior knows that everything and everyone has a story, each uniquely individual. The stories will often change, like the slowly accumulating clouds overhead, always shifting and changing shape, or like raindrops that turn to steam, evaporating and returning again to the clouds.

You hike higher on the mountainous trail watching the ever-changing clouds, reflecting on the impermanence of life.

As the path grows steeper, you notice shapes appearing in the clouds above. A single cloud appears in the shape of an arrowhead. You rub your eyes and look again.

You try to interpret the cloud's message and contemplate the meaning of weapons in general. You know the cloud is symbolic and it makes you think about how people use weapons against each other in daily life.

Words are often people's first weapons of attack. They have the power to destroy an individual's self-esteem and self-worth and can be even more destructive than physical weapons. Warriors never use words in attack because they understand their power and use all of their words wisely.

Warriors don't talk excessively, nor do they interrupt people because they understand that by listening, they learn. Warriors know that everyone they encounter on their journey has the potential to offer wisdom and guidance, and have a story to tell. They listen carefully.

Warriors understand the importance of being quiet each day. They go into silent contemplation and allow their minds to be still, clearing all negative thoughts and words from their minds.

Excessive thoughts are toxic in that they keep people stuck in negative patterns that create fear, self-doubt, and uncertainty.

As a warrior, you know that the words you use to describe your day, your world, and your environment, create your true-life circumstances and manifest in reality.

As you watch the shifting clouds overhead and continue to climb ever higher, the air thins and the elevation changes, causing your breathing to become strained.

You no longer reflect on what was, or what was left behind, but focus on each step, every breath, and the path ahead.

Another cloud appears, this time in the shape of a bear. You are tired, your legs and feet are worn out, your breathing labored, and you want to stop and rest. You are struggling to hike the steep path. Your energy reserves drop drastically. You stop for a rest but in your exhaustion find it difficult to get up again.

As you watch the bear cloud float quietly across the afternoon sky, you reflect on the meaning and symbolism of bears. You know that they represent courage and strength, exactly what you need to get through this next stage of your long journey.

With all of your strength and resolve, and using your newfound walking stick, you slowly stand and continue your journey along the path, following the clouds as they move overhead.

Just as the last cloud disappears from the sky, you reach base camp six, finding yourself nearing the end of your journey to the mountain's summit. You thank the clouds for teaching and guiding you along your way.

The day is almost over as you wander into camp, find your tent, and crawl in, exhausted from your day's journey. You are thankful; you made it through another day and you have learned the lesson of strength.

You will need that lesson of strength more than ever when you continue your journey in the morning.

A Warrior's Checklist

 Strength

We derive strength from many sources. Consider how you might use each of the following to further develop your own personal strength:

- Prayer and reflection
- Physical exercise
- Nutrition
- Motivation
- Goal setting

Base Camp 6

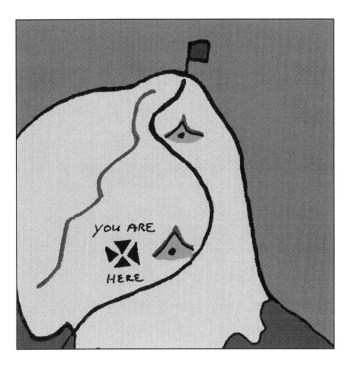

Base Camp 6: Life and Death

Your journey is almost over. In many ways, though, you will discover it is just beginning.

You hear the sound of distant voices as others prepare for their own adventures. Like you, they have made a commitment to change and to become whole.

You know that the next part of the journey will be one of the most difficult, so you pray for guidance and trust that you will arrive safely at the next base camp.

Warriors live in the physical world, yet also walk in the spiritual realm. The true way of the warrior is to navigate both the physical and spiritual worlds with balance.

Warriors know that the path they seek is spirit driven. They do not excessively consume material goods or dwell on physical objects because the journey within enriches their soul in ways that nothing worldly ever can. Over-consumption only weighs down the warrior's progress. Instead they seek to find meaning and happiness in the world around them and in everyday life.

Warriors know that spiritual paths are sacred paths and nothing other than the path ahead is but a distraction to what they seek.

The true journey is ultimately not an external journey, but an internal one that leads the warrior back home to self and spirit.

In the early morning sun, the temperature outside is cold and the air, thin. You are not fully prepared for the extreme weather of the mountain summit but have to rely as best you can on what you have. As in life, we are not always equipped or prepared for what life brings but have to make the most out of difficult or uncomfortable life circumstances.

You take a deep breath of fresh mountain air into your lungs and hold it for a moment, before you breathe out a lifetime of uncertainty.

With your wooden walking stick firmly in hand, you mindfully walk to the trail and observe your surroundings. The path ahead looks steep and treacherous as the mountain plummets steeply at its side.

You take a deep breath and summon the courage to move forward with that ever-important first step. As you hike higher up the side of the mountain, your breathing becomes further strained and the path grows steeper and more dangerous than it has been in previous days. Every step has to be mindful. One false or careless move could cause you to slip and fall off the path and back down the mountain, plunging back into darkness and a life of despair.

You struggle to breathe. You are freezing cold. The wind picks up in intensity making the temperature drop even further, and you begin to doubt that you can make it to the next base camp. Your doubts gather in your mind like dark, foreboding clouds, but you recognize the old, familiar patterns of self-sabotage, and stop those toxic thought patterns because you know you are being tested. When the warrior makes the vow to change and become whole, the universe will conspire to test him or her and will require a regular recommitment to the journey.

The warrior makes the commitment to move through moments of weakness and doubt and uses new-found strength to continue moving forward because this is the way of the warrior.

You press on, toward the summit. After climbing for hours, you search out a place to rest momentarily, but finding nothing, you continue on. The path is changing, becoming rockier and covered with patches of dark, slippery ice. As never before in your journey, you recognize the need for mindfulness—a small mis-step could send you tumbling off the path and into despair.

You stop briefly and look down the mountain and see someone on the path below you. They look ragged and old and you know that they, like you, are struggling on their own personal journey. You wonder how often they have traveled this path alone.

Unable to help them, you turn to face the mountain's summit and keep walking. You take several more steps until you finally see a spot where you can rest. Just as you reach the tiny rock alcove, you slip on a patch of ice and nearly slide off the path to the rocks below. You panic, spiraling your arms in the desperate hope of regaining your balance as you try to grab onto the frozen earth to keep from falling off the path and down the side of the mountain. You find yourself suddenly on your knees, and your hands dig deep into the frozen ground as you try to pull yourself back up. Your arms are sore and trembling from the effort, but you use your remaining strength and slowly pull yourself upright. Just when you get to your feet and reach down for your beloved walking stick, you mis-judge and accidentally knock it over the edge of the path. You watch in horror as it plunges down the side of the mountainside.

The walking stick is gone.

You experience a moment of sadness, but warriors know that attachments are not healthy and always lead to suffering.

With the walking stick gone, you right yourself and look carefully over the edge of the cliff. Trembling, you give thanks that you have not fallen from the path. You see that the person behind you, far below on the trail, has found the stick, and picks it up. You imagine a look of relief on their face. The stick now becomes his companion on his journey. You smile. Although it was your loss, the walking stick is his gain and perhaps much needed on his solo journey. You pray that this warrior's tool will assist the man up the mountain and to his own summit.

Warriors understand that the tools they find and use are temporary, to be shared with others when they no longer serve their own purposes.

The day has been one of the hardest, the climb exhausting, the earlier fall terrifying, but eventually you see base camp seven.

The camp appears isolated and barren, abandoned. Few have made it this far and it looks as though you will be spending the night alone—not far from your goal: the mountain's summit.

You find an empty tent and climb quickly inside. The night air is bitter and freezing cold. You are exhausted. You change your clothes, eat a warm meal, and reflect on the day's lessons.

The past no longer grips you as it did before, but thoughts of how your life will change begin to surface. You stop the thoughts for now, not yet concerned about tomorrow as you live in the present moment. All is well. You have made it further in your journey to the mountain's summit than most. A warrior, you have conquered many obstacles and assembled powerful tools. For now, the journey is enough.

As you begin to fall asleep the wind picks up and rocks your tent, but confident in the journey, and tired, you drift off into a deep sleep.

In the middle of the night, you are abruptly woken as your tent breaks free from the ground. Gale force winds try to rip the tiny canvas tent from beneath your body as you struggle for the zipper in the darkness. The tent quickly smothers your face as you grasp around blindly in the dark, trying to tear yourself from the tent before it pulls you down the mountainside.

Fleetingly, you grab the cold frozen metal zipper, unzip it and quickly crawl out into the raging cold of the storm. The tent flies off into the darkness of the night like a possessed vulture, leaving you frozen, alone, and without shelter in the vanishing mountain air.

You don't know what to do. All of your belongings, your sleeping bag, clothes, and food were all in the tent. Everything is gone. You make your way to a large rock and crowd your shivering body against it, keeping yourself out of the cold wind the best you can. You huddle in place for the rest of the night until the morning sun starts to rise.

Frozen and exhausted, you stand and see that the base camp has been totally wiped out. Nothing remains except scattered debris from previous campers.

You are alone and have nothing. What little you had is gone. You have entered the world of the warrior. You travel with nothing more than a warrior's spirit and a servant's heart.

A Warrior's Checklist

 Personal Attachments

Ask yourself these questions about personal attachments in your life:

- What or who are you attached to?
- How does the attachment serve you?
- How does the attachment cause you pain or suffering?
- Is the attachment healthy?
- Does the attachment serve your higher good or higher purpose?
- If necessary, how can you let go of the attachment?

Base Camp 7

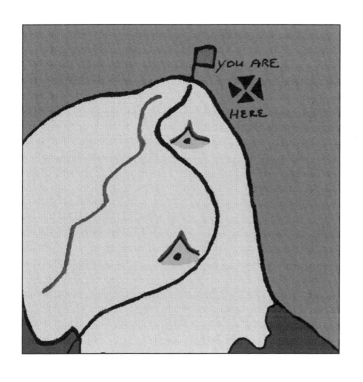

Base Camp 7: The Warrior's Summit

Your last stage of the journey lies ahead, and it will take every ounce of mental and physical strength you have if you are to reach the summit.

You have nothing but the clothes on your back as you search desperately through the debris of the base camp for anything that will assist you in your journey. Luckily you find an old dented water bottle and a heavy woolen coat that were left behind by a previous adventurer. You put the coat on over you own for added warmth and place the water bottle into an exterior pocket. You are grateful for the couple of small swallows of water the bottle contains.

The air is thin, the temperature frigid and you know that the time you have remaining to reach the summit will be limited in such extreme conditions. You have to call upon every bit of your warriors' spirit to help you get to the summit. There is no time to lose.

You continue on the most difficult journey of your lifetime with only thoughts of courage and strength as you take your first step back onto the desolate mountain path.

Although you have almost nothing materially, you are now

spiritually, mentally, and physically equipped to reach the summit.

As the path gains quickly in elevation, the warrior's insight becomes stronger and clearer like the mountain air.

The air thins and the clouds gently disperse, and the warrior can now see what they have left behind, far beneath them; they are no longer pulled by the energy of things left in the past.

Half way up the trail, you spot an ice pick sticking out of the snow. Someone had abandoned their journey, retreating back down the mountain leaving a trail of unwanted items. You are grateful and put the ice pick in your pocket, knowing that you will put it to good use. You are reminded that warriors are always taken care of and that the universe provides them with everything they need, each and every step of the journey.

The wind howls fiercely as you pray for strength to keep moving forward, although every heavy step feels like a thousand steps.

After struggling for what feels like hours, frozen and exhausted, you begin to think that you can't go on. You knew the journey would be difficult, but didn't know it was going to be this hard.

You have thoughts about giving up, when you suddenly hear a loud rumbling noise from above. You look up to see an avalanche with giant shelves of snow and ice sliding down the mountainside close to you. You try to move out of the way, but have nowhere to go.

At the last minute, you remember the ice pick, and force it into a crack in the rock. With the ice pick, you cling to the mountainside trembling in terror as the sheer power and force of the snow wipes out everything around you.

The avalanche stops as abruptly as it started and the mountain is once again silent.

You are stranded alone, with no visible path ahead or behind you. You pray for your life, for your very existence as you can't see your way to the summit and no longer have the option to go back.

Warriors know that life brings challenges to test their strength and courage. This is one of those tests. You swallow your fear and begin to look for a way to the summit, knowing that to remain on the side of the mountain will surely result in death.

With frozen fingers, you pry the pick out of the rock and start to chisel your way up the mountain, inch by inch. The process is painfully hard and progress slow. There are no safety ropes to prevent you from falling. One mis-step will result in a deadly fall. You focus solely on each footstep and the summit ahead, depending only upon yourself and a small ice pick that you are grateful to have found earlier in your journey.

Warriors are tested beyond that of the mortal human. You have made the journey this far and know there is no turning back. The warrior pulls him or herself out of moments of weakness, confident in the strength they have gained along the way. When you make the decision to become whole, nothing will stop or prevent you from fulfilling your mission to becoming your true authentic self, no matter how hard, or difficult the path or obstacles ahead.

With clarity of mind, and a renewed strength, you push onward and upward. You still cannot see the summit due to the steady accumulation of clouds above you, but you know it is there.

With one final step and a mighty push, you suddenly find yourself standing on top of the summit.

A Warrior's Checklist

 Spiritual Path

Reflect upon your spirituality and the role that it plays in your daily life:

- How do you honor your commitment to yourself? How do you do this on a daily basis?
- Have you accepted the call to a spiritual life? If not, what barriers exist? How can you remove them?
- What value in your spiritual path are you willing to share with others?

The Summit

After traveling for what seems a lifetime, you suddenly find yourself standing on top of the mountain's summit.

You have no thoughts, no words to describe the view from the mountain top. The mountain, the summit, holds a sacredness that you have been searching for an entire lifetime.

Even as you have accomplished much, you look at the path below and know instinctively that every day you must climb the mountain yet again. Every climb will be different, though each will become easier as the load you carry will lighten with every trip as you have learned how to navigate your own life.

You sit down next to the purple flag that represents the ending of this adventure and the beginning of your next spiritual journey. You know that others will make the same pilgrimage to wholeness, and you understand that they may benefit if you share your own experiences with them. Physically alone, you come to recognize that you, too, have benefited from others who have made their own journeys before you.

The sun glistens on the snow and although alone in body, you feel more connected to the universe than you ever have before. You feel an overwhelming sense of relief from leaving behind toxic behaviors, patterns, and people. Life will never be the same. Similar issues or problems will still arise, but now you are equipped to address those challenges head on as a warrior.

You sit in a suspended moment of silence on the frozen summit unsure of what lies ahead of you. You want to stay on top of the mountain forever, but you have to go-the summit was never intended as a final destination. Perhaps the temporary nature of the summit is part of its elusive beauty.

You begin to search for a way down but are mindful not to follow the same path as before. Warriors find, create, and build new paths for themselves and for others. You recognize that path building will now be a part of your life's work. As you create those new paths, you will also create maps of words, pictures and experiences, to share with others desiring to make similar journeys in their lives.

Just as you are saying thank you to the mountain for its beautiful yet harsh lessons, you see something glistening in a small patch of ice. One last time, you use the ice pick to chisel a shining, golden object out of the cold ice and see that it is a round, golden talisman in the shape of a medallion. It looks ancient but it also has a familiar image on it.

It is the three triangles, the same image that you saw in the crystalized canyon rock at the beginning of your journey many days ago. It is a symbol of the mountain, representing strength, endurance and achievement.

You hold the golden coin in the palm of your hand knowing that it was placed there for you to find. It is a tangible reminder that you have succeeded in climbing to the summit; you have overcome adversities and now have the strength to make the personal journey to the summit day after day.

You put the sacred talisman in your worn-out coat pocket and turn to begin the long journey back down the mountain side.

As warrior, you encompass the mountains within.

You are the warrior, you will continue to succeed in your everyday climb to the summit, no matter what life's adversities bring: climb, conquer and succeed.

A Warrior's Checklist

Use this as a reminder of the lessons learned from the base camps along your way to the summit.

 Commitment to Change

 Tools for the Journey

 Relapse Prevention

 Vision and Insight

 Strength

 Personal Attachments

 Spiritual Path

THE END

Copyright © 2020 Tomorrow River Publishing

All rights reserved. This book or any portion thereof may not be reproduced or used in any manner whatsoever without the express written permission of the publisher except for the use of brief quotations in a book review.

Printed in the United States of America.

First Edition
First printing, June 2020

Tomorrow River Publishing
1017 Lindbergh Avenue
Stevens Point, WI 54481

www.tomorrowriverpublishing.com

ISBN: 9798655638815

Made in the USA
Middletown, DE
25 October 2020